Collins

AQA GCSE 9-1
Design and Technology

Workbook

Paul Anderson and David Hills-Taylor

Preparing for the GCSE Exam

Revision That Really Works

Experts have discovered that there are two techniques that help you to retain and recall information and consistently produce better results in exams compared to other revision techniques.

It really isn't rocket science either – you simply need to:

- **test yourself** on each topic as many times as possible
- **leave a gap** between the test sessions.

Three Essential Revision Tips

1. Use Your Time Wisely

- Allow yourself plenty of time.
- Try to start revising six months before your exams – it's more effective and less stressful.
- Don't waste time re-reading the same information over and over again – it's not effective!

2. Make a Plan

- Identify all the topics you need to revise.
- Plan at least five sessions for each topic.
- One hour should be ample time to test yourself on the key ideas for a topic.
- Spread out the practice sessions for each topic – the optimum time to leave between each session is about one month but, if this isn't possible, just make the gaps as big as realistically possible.

3. Test Yourself

- Methods for testing yourself include: quizzes, practice questions, flashcards, past papers, explaining a topic to someone else, etc.
- Don't worry if you get an answer wrong – provided you check what the correct answer is, you are more likely to get the same or similar questions right in future!

Visit **collins.co.uk/collinsGCSErevision** for more information about the benefits of these revision techniques, and for further guidance on how to plan ahead and make them work for you.

Command Words used in Exam Questions

This table defines some of the most commonly used command words in GCSE exam questions.

Command word	Meaning
Explain...	Set out purpose or reasons
Name...	Give the correct title or term
State...	Express clearly and briefly
Give...	Produce an answer from recall
Identify...	Name or otherwise characterise
Describe...	Set out characteristics
Complete...	Finish a task by adding to given information

Contents

Design Strategies

1 The table shows three design strategies.

Complete the table by giving **one** advantage and **one** disadvantage of using each design strategy.

Design Approach	Advantage of Strategy	Disadvantage of Strategy
Iterative design		
User-centred design		
Systems thinking		

[6]

Total Marks .... / 6

Electronic Systems

1 The table shows different electronic components.

Complete the table by stating whether each component is an input, process or output device and giving an example application of each in a product.

Component	Input, Process or Output	Application
Push switch		
Lamp		
Microcontroller		
Thermistor		
Buzzer		

[10]

Total Marks _____ / 10

The Work of Others: Designers

1 Name a designer you have studied.

....
[1]

2 State a product that the designer given in your answer to question 1 has designed.

....
[1]

3 Give **four** features of the design given in your answer to question 2.

1 ....

....

2 ....

....

3 ....

....

4 ....

....
[4]

> **Total Marks** .... / 6

The Work of Others: Companies

1 Name a design company that you have studied.

.... [1]

2 State a product that the company given in your answer to question 1 has designed.

.... [1]

3 Give **four** features of the design given in your answer to question 2.

1 ....

....

2 ....

....

3 ....

....

4 ....

.... [4]

Total Marks .... / 6

Ecological, Environmental and Social Issues

1. Explain **three** ways that a product can be designed to be more sustainable.

1 ....

....

....

....

2 ....

....

....

....

3 ....

....

....

.... **[6]**

2. The image shows the Fairtrade Certification mark.

What is meant by the term 'fair trade'?

....

....

....

.... **[2]**

Research and Investigation

1 Explain why designers conduct market research.

....

....

....

.... [2]

2 Explain the purpose of a focus group.

....

....

....

.... [2]

3 Give **two** types of data that can be used when investigating a design problem.

1 ....

2 .... [2]

4 Which of the following is the correct definition of anthropometric data? Tick **one** correct box.

a Height measurements taken from a small sample of people. ☐

b A range of body measurements taken from large numbers of people. ☐

c A range of body measurements taken from a small sample of people. ☐

d Head measurements taken from millions of people. ☐ [1]

Total Marks .... / 7

Briefs and Specifications

1 A design brief for a new product is shown.

> **Design brief**
>
> Young children learn about the world around them through play.
>
> A local company is designing an educational toy aimed at children aged 4–7.
>
> The toy must help the children to improve their literacy skills.

Write a **three**-point design specification for a product that would meet the design brief.

Explain why each point is important.

1 ....

....

Explanation ....

....

....

2 ....

....

Explanation ....

....

....

3 ....

....

Explanation ....

....

.... [6]

Total Marks .... / 6

Exploring and Developing Ideas

1 Sketching ideas can be one stage of an iterative design process.

Give **four** other possible stages of an iterative design process.

1 ....

2 ....

3 ....

4 .... **[4]**

2 The image shows a freehand sketch of a product idea.

Explain why designers produce freehand sketches of ideas for products.

....

....

....

....

....

....

.... **[4]**

Total Marks .... / 8

Communication of Ideas 1

1 State the purpose of an exploded view drawing.

....

.... [1]

2 A company has asked you to design a stand for a mobile phone.

2.1) On the grid, produce an isometric drawing of your design idea. [4]

2.2) Annotate your design to indicate the main features, including:

- the materials and finishes to be used
- how it could be made.

[4]

Total Marks .... / 9

Communication of Ideas 2

1 An alarm system has the following features: when a door is opened, this is detected by a switch. This starts a siren, which stays on for 5 minutes.

Draw a systems diagram for the alarm system, labelling each of the systems blocks and signals.

[12]

2 Explain why a designer may use card to make a physical model of a product.

1 ....

2 .... [2]

Total Marks .... / 14

Computer-Based Tools

1 Tick the correct box. CAD means:

a) Computer-aided drawing ☐

b) Computer-assisted drawing ☐

c) Computer-aided design ☐

d) Computer-assisted drawing ☐ **[1]**

2 Tick the correct box. CAM means:

a) Computer-aided manufacture ☐

b) Computer-assisted manufacture ☐

c) Computer-aided making ☐

d) Computer-assisted making ☐ **[1]**

3 State **four** different ways in which CAD software can be used during the process of developing a product.

1 ....

2 ....

3 ....

4 .... **[4]**

> **Total Marks** .... / 6

Prototype Development

1 State **four** reasons why a designer might make a prototype of a product.

1 ....

....

2 ....

....

3 ....

....

4 ....

....
[4]

2 Explain how a prototype may be different to the final product.

....

....

....

....

....

....

....

....

....

....
[6]

Total Marks .... / 10

Energy Generation and Storage

1 The table shows different sources of energy.

Complete the table by stating whether each is renewable or non-renewable and describing how each is used to produce energy.

Source of Energy	Renewable or Non-Renewable	Description of How Energy is Produced
Tidal		
Coal		

[6]

2 Explain **one** advantage and **one** disadvantage of using nuclear power to generate energy.

Advantage ....

....

....

....

Disadvantage ....

....

....

....

[4]

Total Marks .... / 10

Mechanical Systems 1

1 State which type of motion is represented by each of the following descriptions.

1.1) Moving straight in one direction

.... [1]

1.2) Moving backwards and forwards

.... [1]

1.3) Moving in a circle

.... [1]

1.4) Swinging backwards and forwards

.... [1]

2 **2.1)** State the type of lever shown below.

Load   Effort

Fulcrum   Not to scale

.... [1]

2.2) If the effort required to move a load of 185 N is 37 N, calculate the mechanical advantage of the lever.

....

....

....

.... [2]

Total Marks .... / 7

Mechanical Systems 2

1 Identify a type of linkage that could be used to carry out the following:

1.1) reverse the direction of a linear movement.

_____ [1]

1.2) change the direction of motion by 90°.

_____ [1]

2 State how the following mechanisms change motion:

2.1) cam

_____ [1]

2.2) worm gear

_____ [1]

2.3) rack and pinion

_____ [1]

3 In a simple gear train, when the input gear rotates at a rate of 24 revolutions per minute (rpm) the output gear rotates at 108 rpm.

Calculate the gear ratio.

_____

_____

_____

_____ [2]

Total Marks _____ / 7

Properties of Materials

1 State the meaning of the following properties.

1.1) Hardness

....

.... [1]

1.2) Fusibility

....

.... [1]

2 Complete the table, stating the term described by the first column.

An example has been completed for you.

Description	Term	
the ability of a material to not break when a force is applied to it suddenly	Toughness	
the ability of a material to withstand a force or load that is applied to it	**2.1)**	[1]
the ability of a material to allow heat to pass through it	**2.2)**	[1]
the ability of a material to draw in moisture, light or heat	**2.3)**	[1]

3 Explain the difference between ductility and malleability.

....

....

....

.... [2]

Total Marks .... / 7

Materials: Paper and Board

1 State a typical application for each of the following types of paper and board.

Type of Paper and Board	Typical Application	
Bleed-proof paper	**1.1)**	[1]
Grid paper	**1.2)**	[1]
Duplex board	**1.3)**	[1]
Foil-lined board	**1.4)**	[1]
Foam core board	**1.5)**	[1]

2 Explain **two** reasons why manufacturers use corrugated cardboard to make boxes for packaging.

[4]

Total Marks _____ / 9

Materials: Timber

1 State **two** differences between softwood and hardwood.

1 ....

....

2 ....

....

[2]

2 **2.1)** State **one** reason why natural timber may be seasoned before use.

....

....
[1]

2.2) Describe how timber is seasoned.

....

....

....

....
[2]

3 Explain **two** advantages of manufactured boards over natural timbers.

....

....

....

....

....

....

....
[4]

Total Marks .... / 9

Materials: Metals

1 Explain the difference between ferrous and non-ferrous metals.

....

....

....

.... [2]

2 State a typical application for each of the following types of metal.

Type of Metal	Typical Application	
High-carbon steel	2.1)	[1]
Copper	2.2)	[1]
Aluminium	2.3)	[1]

3 Describe the process involved in making metal from its raw material.

....

....

....

....

....

....

.... [4]

Total Marks .... / 9

Materials: Polymers

1 For each of the polymers listed in the following table, state whether they are thermosetting or thermoforming, and list a typical application.

An example has been completed for you.

Polymer	Thermosetting or Thermoforming	Typical Application
Epoxy resin	*Thermosetting*	*Printed circuit boards*
High-impact polystyrene (HIPS)	a)	b)
Melamine formaldehyde	c)	d)
Polymethyl-methacrylate (PMMA)	e)	f)

[6]

2 A manufacturer is producing water bottles from a polymer. Each bottle is made from 16 g of polymer. The manufacturer has 2.1 m³ of solid polymer, which has a density of 1400 kg m⁻³.

Calculate how many bottles the manufacturer could make. Assume that no material is wasted during the process.

....

....

....

....

....

....

[4]

Total Marks .... / 10

Materials and Their Properties   23

Materials: Textiles

1 Complete the table, identifying whether each fibre is natural or synthetic and giving a typical application.

An example has been completed for you.

Fibre	Natural or Synthetic	Typical Application
Cotton	*Natural*	*Denim jeans*
Lycra		
Wool		
Nylon		
Polyester		
Silk		

[10]

2 Explain why selvedge is important in woven fabrics.

....

.... [2]

Total Marks .... / 12

New Materials

1 Complete the table, listing the 'smart' property of the listed materials and stating an application for which each material is typically used.

Material	Smart Property	Typical Application
Thermochromic pigment		
Photochromic pigment		
Shape memory alloy		

[6]

2 **2.1)** Explain the difference between a composite material and a metal alloy.

[2]

2.2) Name a composite material and give a typical application for which it is used.

[2]

Total Marks _____ / 10

Standard Components

1   Complete the table, naming a different standard component that is used with each material and stating what that component is used for.

An example has been completed for you.

Material	Standard Component	Used for
Metal	*hinge*	*To attach the lid to a metal box*
Fabric		
Timber		
Paper		

[6]

2   Explain why a company may decide to use standard components in a product.

....

....

....

....

....

....

[4]

Total Marks .... / 10

Finishing Materials

1 Give **two** reasons why a finish may be applied to a material.

1 ....

....

2 ....

.... [2]

2 Describe the process of dip-coating a metal product.

....

....

....

....

....

....

....

....

....

....

.... [5]

3 Name a finishing technique used with the following:

3.1) Wood

.... [1]

3.2) Printed circuit boards

.... [1]

Total Marks .... / 9

Selection of Materials

1 Choose **one** of the following products by circling your selection:

Push-along toy for a small child   Swimsuit   Electrical system in a washing machine

Seating in a doctors' waiting room   Cooking pan

Discuss in detail the properties required by the product you have selected.

_____

_____

_____

_____

_____

_____

_____

_____

_____

_____

_____

_____

_____

_____

_____

[9]

Total Marks _____ / 9

Working with Materials

1 Explain **two** reasons why the design of a product may include features to provide reinforcement.

1 ....

....

....

....

2 ....

....

....

....

[4]

2 For each of the following materials, state one method used to change the properties of the material and the effect of that method on the properties.

An example has been completed for you.

Material	How the Properties can be Modified	Effect
Timber	*Seasoning (drying)*	*Reduces risk of warping*
Aluminium		
Polymers		
Fabrics for furniture covers		

[6]

Total Marks .... / 10

Scales of Manufacture

1 Select **one** of the following products:

An alarm circuit   A pair of curtains   Metal garden gates   Wooden wardrobes

A company currently manufactures the product you have selected for individual customers using one-off production. Due to interest from other customers, they are considering introducing batch manufacturing.

Discuss how this change could affect the manufacturing performance of the company.

[10]

Total Marks _____ / 10

Manufacturing Processes 1: Process Types and Processes used with Paper and Board

1 Complete the table below, identifying a **different** tool or process that is typically used to carry out the tasks listed when using paper or card.

An example has been completed for you.

Task	Tool
Cutting or scoring card	*Scissors*
Making a row of small holes in paper so that a part can be torn off easily	a)
Making straight cuts in large pieces of card	b)
Cutting out a complicated 2D net from card when a large quantity is needed	c)
Cutting a small circle in thin card	d)
Using a stencil and ink to apply a design to a one-off banner	e)
Printing large quantities of magazines using multiple colours	f)

[6]

2 **2.1)** Explain what is meant by 'laminating' a paper product.

....

....

....

....

[2]

2.2) Give an example of a laminated product that includes paper or card.

....

[1]

Total Marks .... / 9

1 Identify **two** safety precautions that should be taken when using a wood lathe.

For each, give a reason why it is needed.

Safety Precaution	Reason this is Needed
1.	
2.	

[4]

2 State **two** differences between a tenon saw and a coping saw.

1 ....

....

2 ....

....

[2]

3 Describe how a curved product is made from natural timber by laminating.

....

....

....

....

....

....

....

....

....

[6]

Total Marks .... / 12

Manufacturing Processes 3: Metals and Alloys

1 State **three** methods used to permanently join metal parts together.

1 ....

2 ....

3 .... **[3]**

2 Using notes and/or sketches, describe how a mould is made for sand casting.

[11]

Total Marks .... / 14

Manufacturing Processes 4: Polymers

1 Label the features indicated by arrows on the injection moulding machine below.

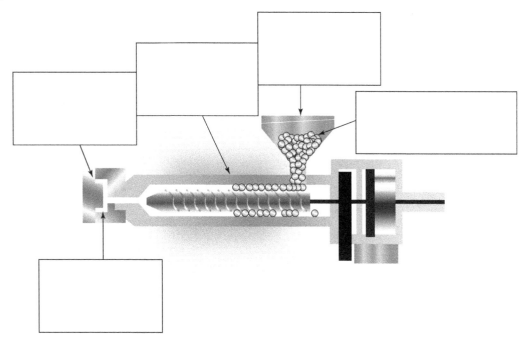

[5]

2 State **two** methods that can be used to make a permanent joint in polymer products.

1 ....

2 .... [2]

3 Give **two** differences between the extrusion and injection moulding processes.

....

....

....

....

....

.... [4]

Total Marks .... / 11

Manufacturing Processes 5: Textiles and Electronic Systems

1 State **two** techniques used to join different pieces of fabric together.

1 ....

2 .... [2]

2 Explain what is meant by 'piping' on a textile product.

....

....

....

....

....

.... [3]

3 State **two** methods used to make printed circuit boards (PCBs).

1 ....

2 .... [2]

4 Explain **two** reasons why reflow (flow) soldering is used to make products in large quantities, rather than manual soldering.

....

....

....

....

....

....

....

.... [6]

Total Marks .... / 13

Measurement and Production Aids

1 State **one** reason why datum points are used when taking measurements.

....

.... **[1]**

2 **2.1)** Describe the purpose of production aids.

....

....

....

.... **[2]**

2.2) Describe **two** different types of patterns that are used in Design and Technology applications.

1 ....

....

2 ....

.... **[4]**

2.3) Other than patterns, name **two** other types of production aids.

1 ....

2 .... **[2]**

> **Total Marks** .... / 9

Ensuring Accuracy

1 State what is meant by the term 'precision'.

_____

_____ [1]

2 Explain **two** ways that accuracy can be improved when manufacturing products.

1 _____

_____

_____

_____

2 _____

_____

_____

_____ [4]

3 Explain the purpose of tolerances in manufacturing.

_____

_____

_____

_____ [2]

Total Marks _____ / 7

Impact on Industry

1 State what is meant by the term 'planned obsolescence'.

....

.... [1]

2 Give **three** benefits of a co-operative business model.

1 ....

....

2 ....

....

3 ....

.... [3]

3 Describe **two** examples of the use of automation in industrial product manufacture.

1 ....

....

....

....

2 ....

....

....

.... [4]

Total Marks .... / 8

Impact on Production

1 Describe **one** example of market pull and **one** example of technology push.

Market pull

_____

_____

_____

_____

Technology push

_____

_____

_____

_____

[4]

2 **2.1)** Give **three** advantages of using CAD software over producing drawings by hand.

1 _____

_____

2 _____

_____

3 _____

[3]

2.2) Explain **one** disadvantage of manufacturing products with CAM equipment over production using manual methods.

_____

_____

_____

[2]

Total Marks _____ / 9

Impact on Society and the Environment

1 Describe **two** examples of inclusive design.

1 ....

....

....

....

2 ....

....

....

....

[4]

2 Describe, using an example, what is meant by a finite resource.

....

....

....

....

[2]

3 State **two** examples of cultural issues that should be considered when designing products.

1 ....

....

2 ....

[2]

Total Marks .... / 8

Collins

GCSE
Design and Technology

Time allowed: 2 hours

Materials

For this paper you must have:

- writing and drawing instruments
- a calculator
- a protractor.

Instructions

- Use black ink or black ball-point pen. Use pencils only for drawing.
- Answer **all** questions.
- Answer the questions in the spaces provided. Do not write on blank pages.
- Do all your work in this book. Cross through any work you do not want to be marked.

Information

- The marks for questions are shown in brackets.
- The maximum mark for this paper is 100.
- There are 20 marks for Section A, 30 marks for Section B and 50 marks for Section C.

Name: ....

Practice Exam Paper

Section A

Questions **1–10** are multiple choice questions. You must shade in one lozenge.

1   Which one of the following sources of energy is a fossil fuel?

    A   biomass   ◯

    B   nuclear   ◯

    C   oil   ◯

    D   solar   ◯   **[1 mark]**

2   What does the term 'fusibility' describe?

    A   the ability of a material to burn   ◯

    B   the ability of a material to melt when heated   ◯

    C   the ability of a material to provide electrical resistance   ◯

    D   the ability of a material to be stretched without breaking   ◯   **[1 mark]**

3 Which one of the following is a ferrous metal?

A aluminium ⬜

B copper ⬜

C tin ⬜

D tool steel ⬜ [1 mark]

4 What type of motion is shown in Figure 1?

Figure 1

A linear ⬜

B oscillating ⬜

C reciprocating ⬜

D rotary ⬜ [1 mark]

5 Which one of the following is a synthetic fibre?

A cotton ◯

B polyamide ◯

C silk ◯

D wool ◯ **[1 mark]**

6 Which type of paper is commonly used for leaflets, as it resists inks and colours seeping through it?

A bleed-proof paper ◯

B cartridge paper ◯

C grid paper ◯

D grid paper ◯ **[1 mark]**

7 Which one of the following best describes market pull?

A advertising to increase the number of customers for a product ◯

B prices for products being reduced over time ◯

C products being produced due to new technologies becoming available ◯

D the development of new products due to consumer demand ◯ **[1 mark]**

8 A designer is developing a system to automatically open a door when someone stands on a pressure sensor. What type of component is a pressure sensor?

A input ○

B process ○

C programmable ○

D output ○ [1 mark]

9 A new product includes a removable cover so that the batteries can be replaced when they run out. This is an example of:

A anthropometric design ○

B design for maintenance ○

C flexible manufacturing ○

D planned obsolescence ○ [1 mark]

1 0 Which one of the following is a softwood?

A balsa ○

B mahogany ○

C oak ○

D pine ○ [1 mark]

Practice Exam Paper

1 1 · 1 Figure 2 shows a simple gear train.

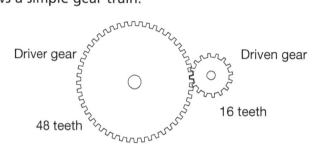

Driver gear

Driven gear

48 teeth

16 teeth

Figure 2

Calculate the gear ratio of this gear train.

[2 marks]

1 1 · 2 Give **two** examples of a third-order lever.

1

2

[2 marks]

1 2 · 1 Name a smart material.

[1 mark]

`1` `2` · `2` For the material you have named in 12.1, state the property that makes it a smart material.

_____

_____

_____

[1 mark]

`1` `3` Figure 3 shows a fork made from stainless steel.

Figure 3

State **two** reasons why forks are often made from stainless steel.

1 _____

2 _____

[2 marks]

`1` `4` Describe briefly how electricity is generated using nuclear power.

_____

_____

_____

_____

_____

[2 marks]

Practice Exam Paper

Section B

1 5 Choose one product or component from Figure 4.

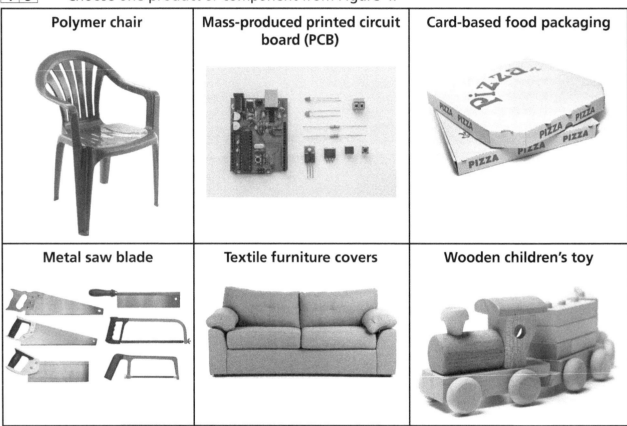

Polymer chair	Mass-produced printed circuit board (PCB)	Card-based food packaging
Metal saw blade	Textile furniture covers	Wooden children's toy

Figure 4

Name of product: ....

1 5 · 1 Explain how the material could be modified to improve one property or characteristic of this product.

....

....

....

....

....

....

....

....

....

....

[4 marks]

1 5 · 2 For the product you have chosen, explain how **two** of the 6 Rs can be used to make the product more sustainable.

1 ....

....

....

....

2 ....

....

....

....

[4 marks]

1 6 Describe the typical characteristics of the following types of production.

1 6 · 1 Mass production

....

....

....

....

....

....

....

[3 marks]

1 6 · 2 Batch production

_____

_____

_____

_____

_____

[2 marks]

1 6 · 3 Prototype production

_____

_____

_____

_____

_____

[2 marks]

1 7 Choose **one** of the products listed in Table 1.

A monthly magazine	The wheel for a child's toy, made from wood	A block of metal with a milled slot	A template made from laser-cut polymer	Curtains with a printed repeating design	A printed circuit board (PCB)

Table 1

Name of product/component: _____

17 · 1 Describe a quality control system that may be used during the manufacture of your chosen product.

[3 marks]

17 · 2 The part you have chosen has one feature with a dimension of 45 mm and a tolerance of 2 mm. Calculate the acceptable maximum and minimum sizes of the feature.

[2 marks]

1 8 Companies often consider social issues when designing and manufacturing products. These may include, for example, working conditions, pollution and the impact of the product and its manufacture on others.

Evaluate how the consideration of social issues may affect the design and manufacture of products.

_____

_____

_____

_____

_____

_____

_____

_____

_____

_____

_____

_____

_____

_____

_____

Continue your answer on a separate piece of paper.   **[10 marks]**

Section C

Figure 5 shows a mobile phone designed to help elderly people communicate with friends and family members.

Figure 5

Specification:

- Lightweight and portable
- Simple function – text messages and phone calls only
- Large buttons
- Battery powered

Practice Exam Paper

1 9 Study the mobile phone and the information shown on the previous page.

1 9 . 1 Choose **two** of the specification points given. For each, explain why it was included.

Specification point 1: ....

Explanation ....

....

....

Specification point 2: ....

Explanation ....

....

....

[4 marks]

1 9 . 2 Explain **one** improvement that would make the phone more suitable for the target audience.

....

....

....

....

....

....

....

....

[3 marks]

1 9 · 3 Explain how the design of the phone would need to be modified if the target audience was changed to teenagers.

....

....

....

....

....

....

....

....

....

....

[4 marks]

2 0 The mobile phone shown on page 213 is powered by a battery. The company collected data on how long the batteries lasted before they needed replacing, see Table 2. Data was recorded for 50 products.

No battery needed replacing in less than 50 hours. All of the batteries needed replacing in less than 150 hours.

Battery life, hours	50 < 70	70 < 90	90 < 110	110 < 130	130 < 150
Cumulative total number of failed batteries	1	5	14	30	50

Table 2

2 0 · 1 Produce a line graph of the cumulative battery life.

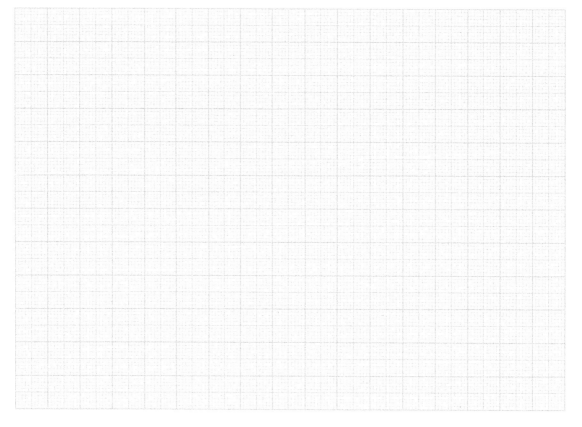

[5 marks]

2 0 · 2 Calculate the mean average number of hours for the life of the batteries.

[2 marks]

2 0 · 3 Determine the time at which 50% of the batteries needed to be replaced.

[2 marks]

2 0 · 4 Explain the difference between the values calculated in 20.2 and 20.3.

[2 marks]

Page 36 Measurement and Production Aids

1. To provide reference points for the measurements [1]
2. 2.1) To provide accuracy [1] and precision of production [1].
   2.2) Textile/fabric patterns [1] which are used to trace parts of a garment onto fabric before it is cut [1]. Casting patterns for metal/plastic resin [1] which are used to prepare a cavity for pouring in the molten material [1].
   2.3) Jigs [1], templates [1]

Page 37 Ensuring Accuracy

1. How repeatable/reproducible a measurement is [1].
2. Increased use of CAD/CAM equipment [1] as computerised equipment is more accurate than human operators [1]. Use of jigs/templates [1] as these can be used to hold a material/guide cutting tools [1].
3. To give the permissible level of variation in the dimensions of a manufactured product [1] so that issues such as improper fits/wasted materials/non-functioning products are avoided [1].

Page 38 Impact on Industry

1. A business strategy where a product is designed to be no longer useful after a set period of time [1].
2. Can be set up by just a small number of people [1], benefits from buying power of whole membership [1], all members share in the profits made [1].
3. Award 1 mark each for up to four of the following points: Use of automated robotic arms [1] for assembling products on a production line [1]. Use of automated sensor systems [1] for detecting defects in manufactured products [1]. Use of CAM/CNC equipment [1] for cutting materials to shape/size [1].

Page 39 Impact on Production

1. Market pull: The development of the digital camera [1] which has become smaller/lighter/better performing as a result of customer wants/needs [1].
   Technology push: Smartphones/tablet computers [1] which were developed as a result of improvements in touch screen technology [1].
2. 2.1) Award 1 mark each for up to three of the following points: Greater accuracy [1], ease of modification [1], reduced storage requirements [1], ease of sharing digitally [1], can be exported to CAM/CNC equipment [1], drawings can be automatically produced from 3D models [1], designs can be simulated [1].
   2.2) High setup costs [1] which can be prohibitive to businesses with small turnovers/manufacturing quotas [1].

Page 40 Impact on Society and the Environment

1. Award 1 mark each for up to two of the following points: A phone with large buttons [1] designed for use by elderly people [1]. A garden tool with an ergonomic handle [1] for people who suffer from arthritis [1]. A door with a handle that can be pulled from different heights [1] that can be used by people in wheelchairs and/or children as well as adults [1].
2. A resource that will eventually run out [1], for example fossil fuels/metals/oil-based plastics/woods from trees that are not replaced [1].
3. Award 1 mark each for up to two of the following points: Religious preferences/faiths/beliefs [1], current trends [1], use/meaning of colour [1], use/meaning of language [1], different meanings of logos/symbols [1].

Pages 42–47 Practice Exam Paper Section A

1. C [1]
2. B [1]
3. D [1]
4. B [1]
5. B [1]
6. A [1]
7. D [1]
8. A [1]
9. B [1]
10. D [1]
11. 11.1) Gear ratio = number of teeth on driven gear / number of teeth on driver gear. Gear ratio = 16:48 [1] Reducing to lowest common denominator, Gear ratio = 1:3 [1]
    Note: this must be presented as a ratio. The answer mark will not be awarded for a decimal value, i.e. 0.33.
    11.2) 1 mark each for two suitable examples, for example: a broom, a fishing rod, a pair of tweezers, a spade/shovel, a hammer.
12. 12.1) 1 mark each for two suitable examples, for example: shape memory alloys, thermochromic pigments, photochromic pigments.
    12.2) 1 mark for stating the smart property of the material named in 12.1, for example: returns to original shape when heated, changes colour with temperature, changes colour with changes in the level of light, respectively.
13. 1 mark each for two suitable reasons. For example: resistant to corrosion, non-toxic/will not taint food, can be reused, strength/doesn't bend when used, can be placed in a dishwasher. Any other appropriate answer.
14. The nuclear pile generates heat/turns water into steam [1]. The steam turns a generator, producing electricity [1].

Pages 48–52 Practice Exam Paper Section B

15. 15.1) 1 mark for identifying the property modified, 1 mark for stating how it could be modified and up to 2 marks for detail about the modification or reasons why it is modified. For example, polymer chair – improved durability [1] by adding stabilisers to resist UV degradation [1] as this stops sunshine weakening the polymer [1] as it is used outside [1]. Mass-produced PCB – minimising cost [1] by the use of photosensitive board [1] to enable rapid production [1] of complex designs [1]. Card-based food packaging – reduced absorbency [1] by the use of additives to prevent moisture transfer [1] so that the packaging does not become soggy [1] when it contains hot food that gives off moisture [1]. Metal saw blade – heat treatment [1] to prevent brittleness of the blade [1] whilst keeping a hard cutting edge [1], enabling a lower cost material to be used [1]. Textile furniture covers – reduce flammability [1] by treating with flame retardants [1] to minimise risk of home fires [1] if it is accidentally set alight by a cigarette or electrical spark [1]. Wooden children's toy – improved dimensional stability [1] by seasoning [1] to reduce the moisture content [1] in case the wood is stored outside in the rain [1]. Note: the use of different surface finishes with appropriate detail and reasons will also be awarded marks.
    15.2) 1 mark each for stating two of the 6 Rs and 1 mark each for explaining how the chosen product could be modified and the implications of this modification. For example, reuse [1] – such as giving the wooden toy to a different child when the initial child grows older and loses interest in it [1]. Recycle [1] – such as melting down old saw blades so that they can be used in new products [1]. Rethink [1] – such as creating multi-use packaging rather than disposable food packaging [1]. Reduce [1] – such as making textile furniture covers that only cover the visible parts of the furniture (i.e. not the back). Refuse [1] – such as buying chairs made from sustainable material rather than polymers [1]. Repair [1] – such as using standard parts on the PCB to allow replacements when it fails [1].
16. 16.1) Up to 3 marks for details such as: very large number of products produced [1] often using a production line [1]. This can involve high use of CAM (computer-aided manufacture) equipment [1] and sub-assemblies [1].

16.2) Up to 2 marks for details such as: fixed quantity of identical products manufactured [1]; jigs and templates often used to aid production [1]; flexible machines that can be changed over to produce different products [1].

16.3) Up to 2 marks for details such as: manufacture of a bespoke single item [1] typically by highly skilled workers [1]; flexible machines that may be manually controlled [1].

17. 17.1) Award up to 3 marks for identifying an appropriate quality control system and giving details about its implementation. For example, monthly magazine – use of registration marks [1]. These are printed outside the trim area of printing [1] and allow the printer to accurately align separate press plates for multi-colour print jobs [1]. Wooden wheel – go/no-go gauge [1]. If the wheel fits between the maximum indicators, it is less than the maximum tolerance [1]; if it does not fit between the markers for the minimum size, it is above the minimum tolerance [1]. Slotted metal block – using a depth-stop [1] pre-set to the required depth [1] with machining stopping when the depth-stop contacts the material [1]. Polymer template – selecting the correct laser settings [1], such as % power [1] and cutting speed [1]. Curtains – using an original sample/master [1] to check the dimensions of the repeat print [1] and its colour [1]. PCB – controlling times for UV exposure [1], developing [1] and etching [1].

17.2) 43 mm [1] and 47 mm [1]

18. 9–10 marks: excellent understanding shown and points well evaluated in depth. Appropriate and fully justified conclusions presented. 7–8 marks: good understanding shown and points well evaluated. Appropriate conclusions presented with some justification. 5–6 marks: good understanding shown with some points evaluated. Appropriate but unjustified conclusions presented. 3–4 marks: some understanding shown. Limited evaluation. Limited conclusions made. 1–2 marks: few points made or one point made with some limited explanation. No conclusion. 0 marks: no response worthy of merit. Indicative content: use the following as points for further evaluation to demonstrate understanding. If other valid responses are presented, they should also be given full credit. Working conditions – conformance of factories to safety legislation and standards; legal and ethical implications of non-compliance; how conformance may vary between countries; effect on the manufacturing cost. Pollution – impact on marine/local habitats; potential for contamination of the food chain; potential options for reducing pollution and how these may affect the design and manufacture of products; disposal of products at the end of their life. Impacts on others – potential negative impacts; consideration of social footprint, ethical issues and the materials used in products; influence on the wider society. Whilst candidates can answer in general terms, responses may include specific examples of products – credit will be awarded if these are appropriate.

Pages 53–62 Practice Exam Paper Section C

19. 19.1) 1 mark for each relevant point of explanation, up to maximum of 2 marks per specification point chosen. For example, simple function – no unnecessary features [1], making it easier for someone not confident with technology to use the phone [1]. Large buttons – easier for elderly people to see the buttons/numbers [1] so suitable for users with poor eyesight [1]; easier to press [1] so suitable for people with arthritis, etc. [1].

19.2) 1 mark for identifying a relevant improvement and up to 2 marks for explaining how it would make the phone more suitable. For example, the phone could be given a more ergonomic shape [1]. This would make it easier to grip [1] and therefore reduce fatigue during use [1].

19.3) 1 mark for each suitable point relating to colour, shape, screen size/type, features of the phone, etc. up to a maximum of 4 marks. For example, including additional features on the phone such as multiple cameras [1] and WiFi access [1]. Increasing the memory [1] so that it can hold apps [1]. Making it a brighter colour [1] so that it is more attractive to teenage buyers [1]. Including a larger screen [1] so that they can see more detail when running apps or looking at social media [1]. Having touch-sensitive capability [1] to allow data input or selection of options [1].

20. 20.1) 1 mark for making the battery life the x axis and the total number of failed batteries the y axis; 1 mark for appropriate range of values for the axes; 1 mark for a line starting at 50,0; 1 mark for points plotted at the top end of each band (70, 90, 110, 130, 150); 1 mark for a line approximating to the correct shape.

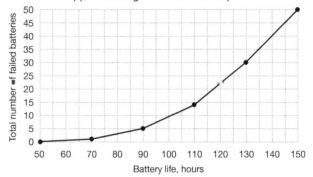

20.2) Average value = ((1 × 60) + (4 × 80) + (9 × 100) + (16 × 120) + (20 × 140))/50 [1] = 120 hours [1]

20.3) 50% of the batteries = 25 batteries [1] Reading from the graph, this equates to a battery life of 124 hours [1].

20.4) The relationship is exponential [1], so the halfway point on the graph (50% of components) is lower than the average [1].

21. 21.1) 1 mark for each advantage up to a maximum of 2 marks and 1 mark for an explanation of each up to a maximum of 2 marks. For example, the finished product is more likely to meet user expectations [1] because their needs are considered at all stages [1]. Users have more ownership of the final product [1] meaning they will be more likely to buy it [1].

21.2) 1 mark for each disadvantage up to a maximum of 2 marks. For example, takes longer to design the products [1]. Increased expense of implementing suggested changes [1]. Can result in products that are only suited to certain users [1].

21.3) 1 mark for each suitable point up to a maximum of 2 marks, such as: an approach used to present a top-down overview of systems [1] by splitting them into input, process and output blocks [1], uses block/systems diagrams to communicate ideas [1]

22. 22.1) 1 mark for correct working and 1 mark for correct answer: A = 155 / (tan 30°) [1] A = 268.5 mm [1]

22.2) 1 mark for each suitable point up to a maximum of 2 marks: to provide a reference point/surface [1] from which measurements can then be taken [1].

22.3) 1 mark for each valid method up to a maximum of 2 marks, such as: nesting [1], use of jigs/patterns/templates [1].

23. 23.1) 1 mark for each valid response up to a maximum of 2 marks. For example, papers and boards – printing [1], embossing [1], UV varnishing [1]; Timbers – painting [1], varnishing [1], tanalising [1], painting [1], waxing [1]; Metals – dip-coating [1], powder coating [1], galvanising [1], painting [1]; Polymers – polishing [1], printing [1], application of vinyl decals [1]; Textiles – printing [1], applying dyes and stain protection [1]; Systems – PCB lacquering [1], lubrication [1]

23.2) 1 mark for each valid reason up to a maximum of 2 marks, such as: for visual/aesthetic reasons **[1]**, to protect against corrosion/oxidation/wear/damage, etc. **[1]**

23.3) 1 mark for each point describing or showing the application of the surface treatment or finish, up to a maximum of 5 marks. For example, varnishing timber – sand wood to create a smooth surface **[1]**, apply filler to any holes **[1]**, use a brush to apply wood sealer or primer **[1]**, apply the varnish **[1]**, add additional coats as necessary **[1]**, allow sufficient time for each coat to dry **[1]**. Galvanising steel – clean the steel **[1]**, place in a molten zinc bath **[1]** of around 460° **[1]**, hold until the steel reaches the desired temperature **[1]** and the bond between the steel and zinc is formed **[1]**, quench the steel **[1]**. Applying vinyl decals to polymer – use a craft knife/vinyl cutter to cut the decals **[1]** from the vinyl sheet **[1]**, peel off the decals from the paper backing **[1]**, position accurately on the plastic surface **[1]**, ensure pressed smoothly onto the plastic surface **[1]**.

24.1) 1 mark for each suitable point up to a maximum of 2 marks: when a designer is not able to move past the first design idea/does not explore the full range of design options **[1]**, leading to potentially good design solutions being missed **[1]**.

24.2) 1 mark for each suitable point up to a maximum of 3 marks, such as: to test how the product/system would work **[1]**; to show to users/clients **[1]** so they can suggest improvements **[1]**; to see how the product would look in 3D **[1]**; to spot errors in the design **[1]** so they can be corrected before manufacturing of the final product/system begins **[1]**.

Notes

ACKNOWLEDGEMENTS

The author and publisher are grateful to the copyright
holders for permission to use quoted materials and images.

All images © Shutterstock.com

Every effort has been made to trace copyright holders and obtain their
permission for the use of copyright material. The author and publisher
will gladly receive information enabling them to rectify any error or omis-
sion in subsequent editions. All facts are correct at time of going to press.

Published by Collins
An imprint of HarperCollins*Publishers* Ltd
1 London Bridge Street
London SE1 9GF

HarperCollins*Publishers*
1st Floor, Watermarque Building, Ringsend
Road, Dublin 4, Ireland

© HarperCollins*Publishers* Limited 2022

ISBN 9780008535063

This edition published 2022

10 9 8 7 6 5 4 3 2 1

British Library Cataloguing in Publication Data.

A CIP record of this book is available from the British Library.

Authored by: Paul Anderson and David Hills-Taylor
Project management and editorial: Nik Prowse and Shelley Teasdale
Commissioning: Katherine Wilkinson, Clare Souza and Katie Galloway
Cover Design: Kevin Robbins and Sarah Duxbury
Inside Concept Design: Sarah Duxbury and Paul Oates
Text Design and Layout: Jouve India Private Limited
Production: Lyndsey Rogers
Printed and bound in the UK using 100% Renewable
Electricity at CPI Group (UK) Ltd

MIX
Paper from
responsible source
FSC˚ C007454

This book is produced from independently
certified FSC™ paper to ensure responsible
forest management.

For more information visit:
www.harpercollins.co.uk/green